FRIENDS & FAMILY™

MERIT  BADGES

FOR THOSE WHO MATTER MOST

TEACHERS

FRIENDS

AUNTS

NIECES

UNCLES

NEPHEWS

NEIGHBORS

BABYSITTERS

STUDENTS

YOUTH CLUBS

COUSINS

DISCONNECT FROM THE DIGITAL© AND CONNECT WITH THOSE WHO MATTER MOST.

For More Information:
DCGifts Online, LLC
feedback@grandparentmeritbadges.com

Halo Publishing International
7550 WIH-10 #800, PMB 2069,
San Antonio, TX 78229

Second Edition, August 2023
ISBN: 978-1-63765-469-9
LCCN: 2023914016

Halo Publishing International is a self-publishing company that publishes adult fiction and non-fiction, children's literature, self-help, spiritual, and faith-based books. Do you have a book idea you would like us to consider publishing? Please visit www.halopublishing.com for more information.

FRIENDS & FAMILY™
MERIT BADGES

Throughout the world today – across the United States, Asia, Europe, and all corners of the globe – people are looking for a way to DISCONNECT FROM THE DIGITAL™ and spend more time with those who matter most. Friends and family members of all kinds – you name it – Aunts, Uncles, Nieces, Nephews, Cousins, Brothers, Sisters, Friends, Neighbors, Babysitters, even Teachers and Students, are finding new ways to spend more in person time with each other doing all sorts of fun things.

To DISCONNECT FROM THE DIGITAL™, means becoming consciously aware of how much time is being spent using technology to surf the internet, scroll through social media apps, or playing digital online games (all things that take us out of the here and now with our loved ones!), and then purposefully refocusing on activities that allow us to reconnect with the people in our lives that matter most to us.

Friends and family who are fortunate enough to live near one another know what joy spending a little personal time together can bring. Being able to do things together is especially valuable for friends and family that live in different cities, states, or even countries. Video calls and visual connection applications like Facime™, Zoom™, Skype™, etc. are great technology tools that can be used for reconnecting with the important people in our lives who aren't physically near us. Use these kinds of tools to reach out and spend some "face" time together when you can't physically be in the same place.

The activities in the Friends and Family Merit Badges™ book can be modified so all types of participants can still have fun spending time and earning merit badges together. Whether it be in person or remotely! For instance, you can experience a zoo or aquarium by visiting their website together while you visit on the phone. Or, take pictures in each of your respective locations and then schedule a video call to share your experiences with each other. Compare the similarities and differences between the two locations you visited. Be creative and have fun coming up with new ways to connect with your family and friends!

Additionally, when it comes to disconnecting from the digital and reconnecting with loved ones, everyone counts...young, middle-aged, or old, those with special needs, or those who need some additional physical assistance to get around. Most libraries, zoos, aquariums, parks, and museums around the country have made great strides in accommodating those with special needs following the adoption of the Americans with Disabilities Act ("ADA"). Check them out. You may be pleasantly surprised at what you find. And many of the activities in this book don't require any special event or venue. Just the desire to spend time together just about anywhere!

Taking a walk, reading a book, riding a bike, cooking a meal...the simplest pleasures in life are becoming more important to our wellbeing each day. These kinds of simple activities are an opportunity for friends and family members to talk, discover, play, and grow together. Disconnecting from the digital and reconnecting with those that matter most all started with the Grandparent Merit Badges™ kits. They were so popular, people other than Grandparents asked, "What About Us?!". They sought their own version for friends and other family members to use. The Friends and Family Merit Badges™ is simply a celebration and recognition of the thousands of things millions of people do together every day.

DISCONNECT FROM THE DIGITAL™ and reconnect with those that matter most!

Start enjoying the Friends and Family Merit Badges™ today!

THIS BELONGS TO:

Find the Aquarium Badge and Place It Here!

Where? _______________________

Date Completed: _____________

What Did You See?

____

____

____

____

Place or Draw A Picture Showing Your Fun Day Here!

Where? ___________________________

Date Completed: _______________

Describe the Cookies:

____

____

____

____

Find the Cookies Badge and Place It Here!

Where? ___________________

Date Completed: ____________

What Sport Did You Play?

____

____

____

____

Place or Draw A Picture Showing Your Fun Day Here!

Where? _______________________

Date Completed: _______________

What Is the Puzzle Picture?

____

____

____

____

**Find the Puzzle Badge
and Place It Here!**

Place or Draw A Picture Showing Your Fun Day Here!

RIDE A BIKE

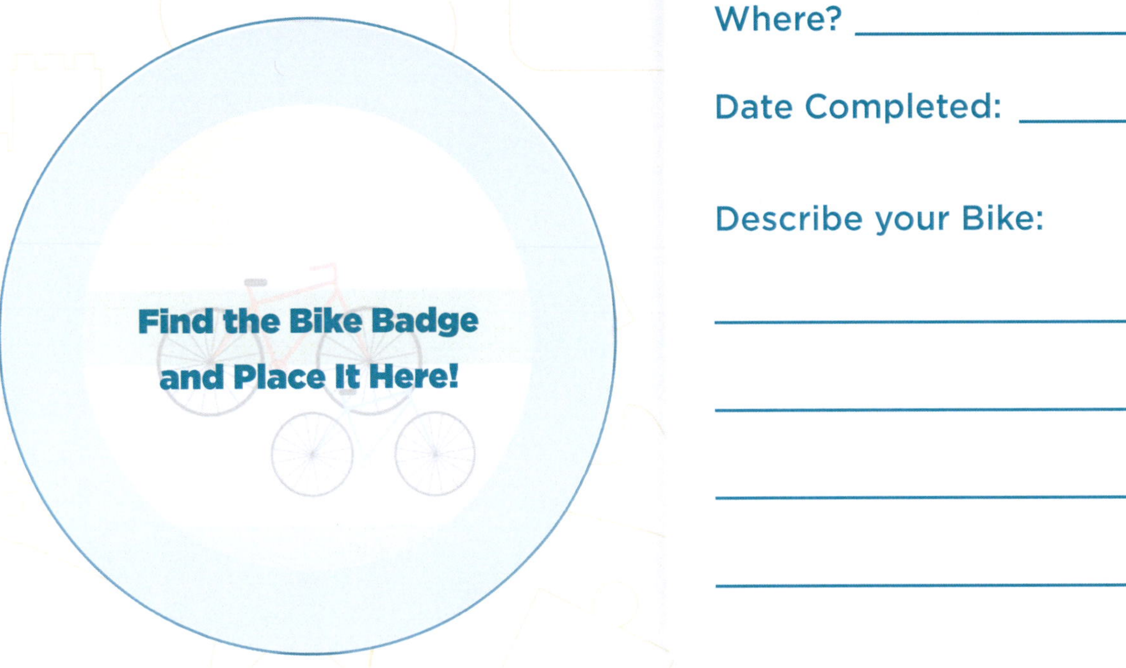

Where? ___________________

Date Completed: ___________

Describe your Bike:

____

____

____

____

Place or Draw A Picture Showing Your Fun Day Here!

Where? _______________________

Date Completed: ____________

Describe Your Favorite Picture

You Took:

____

____

____

**Find the Camera Badge
and Place It Here!**

Place or Draw A Picture Showing Your Fun Day Here!

Find the Fishing Badge and Place It Here!

Where? _______________________

Date Completed: _______________

Describe the Fish You Caught:

____

____

____

____

Place or Draw A Picture Showing Your Fun Day Here!

Where? _____________________

Date Completed: _____________

Describe Your Kite:

____

____

____

____

**Find the Kite Badge
and Place It Here!**

Find the Letter Badge and Place It Here!

Where? ____________________

Date Completed: ____________

How Long Did it Take the Letter to Get There?

____

____

____

 Place or Draw A Picture Showing Your Fun Day Here!

PLANT A GARDEN

Where? _______________________

Date Completed: _______________

What Did You Plant?

____

____

____

____

**Find the Garden Badge
and Place It Here!**

Find the Family Tree Badge and Place It Here!

Where? ___________________________

Date Completed: ______________

What Did You Learn?

____

____

____

____

Place or Draw A Picture Showing Your Fun Day Here!

HAVE A MEAL TOGETHER

Where? _____________________

Date Completed: ______________

What Did You Eat?

____

____

____

____

**Find the Meal Badge
and Place It Here!**

Find the Swimming Badge
and Place It Here!

Where? _______________________

Date Completed: _____________

Describe the Weather Today:

____

____

____

____

Place or Draw A Picture Showing Your Fun Day Here!

Where? ___________________________

Date Completed: ______________

What Movie Did You See?

____

____

____

____

Find the Movie Badge
and Place It Here!

Place or Draw A Picture Showing Your Fun Day Here!

Find the Zoo Badge and Place It Here!

Where? _______________________

Date Completed: _______________

What Is Your Favorite Animal?

____

____

____

____

Place or Draw A Picture Showing Your Fun Day Here!

Book Title: _______________

Date Completed: __________

What Was the Book About?

____

____

____

____

Find the Book Badge and Place It Here!

Place or Draw A Picture Showing Your Fun Day Here!

Find the Video Chat Badge and Place It Here!

Where? ___________________________

Date Completed: _______________

Where Were Each of You?

____

____

____

____

Place or Draw A Picture Showing Your Fun Day Here!

Where? _______________________

Date Completed: ___________

What Was the Walk Like?

____

____

____

____

**Find the Walking Badge
and Place It Here!**

Draw Your Own Activity Here!!

Where? _______________________

Date Completed: ____________

What Did You See?

____

____

____

____

 Place or Draw A Picture Showing Your Fun Day Here!

____

Where? _____________________

Date Completed: ____________

Describe Your Activity:

____

____

____

____

Draw Your Own Activity Here!!

Certificate of Merit

This certifies that ________________________("Friend/Family Member")
and ________________________("Friend/Family Member")
completed _____ of the Friends and Family Merit Badges™.

This Certificate of Merit celebrates the relationship between them.

Certified this ________ day of ________________, 20___.

____
Name/Relation/Friend

____
Name/Relation/Friend

With the help of an adult, cut around the dotted lines of the right merit badge with scissors and then glue (or tape) the merit badge on the right journal page once you have completed that activity.

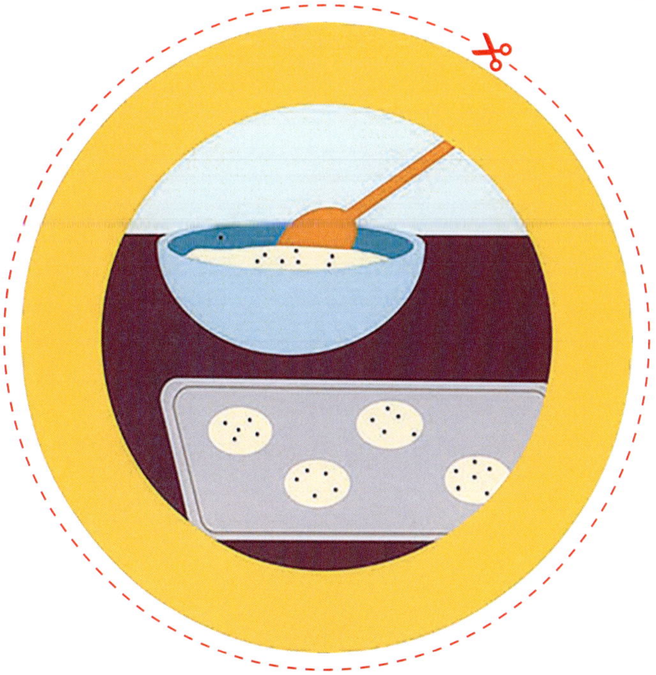

With the help of an adult, cut around the dotted lines of the right merit badge with scissors and then glue (or tape) the merit badge on the right journal page once you have completed that activity.

With the help of an adult, cut around the dotted lines of the right merit badge with scissors and then glue
(or tape) the merit badge on the right journal page once you have completed that activity.

Printed by BoD™in Norderstedt, Germany